MEXICO
BEAUTIFUL LAND
DIVERSE PEOPLE

MEXICAN ART AND ARCHITECTURE

ANNA CAREW-MILLER

The unique and colorful character of Mexico can be seen even in everyday details. This metal doorknocker in the shape of a face was created with painstaking effort, as well as plenty of creativity.

MEXICO
BEAUTIFUL LAND
DIVERSE PEOPLE

MEXICAN ART AND ARCHITECTURE

ANNA CAREW-MILLER

Mason Crest Publishers
Philadelphia

Produced by OTTN Publishing, Stockton, N.J.

Mason Crest Publishers
370 Reed Road
Broomall PA 19008
www.masoncrest.com

First Printing

1 3 5 7 9 8 6 4 2

Library of Congress Cataloging-in-Publication Data

Carew-Miller, Anna.
    Mexican art & architecture / Anna Carew-Miller.
        p. cm. — (Mexico—beautiful land, diverse people)
    Includes bibliographical references and index.
    ISBN 978-1-4222-0656-0 (hardcover) — ISBN 978-1-4222-0723-9 (pbk.)
    1. Arts, Mexican—Juvenile literature. I. Title. II. Title: Mexican art and architecture.
    NX514.A1F55 2008
    700.972—dc22

                                    2008031856

TABLE OF CONTENTS

MEXICO
BEAUTIFUL LAND
DIVERSE PEOPLE

THE ECONOMY OF MEXICO

FAMOUS PEOPLE OF MEXICO

THE FESTIVALS OF MEXICO

THE FOOD OF MEXICO

THE GEOGRAPHY OF MEXICO

THE GOVERNMENT OF MEXICO

THE HISTORY OF MEXICO

MEXICAN ART AND ARCHITECTURE

THE PEOPLE OF MEXICO

SPORTS OF MEXICO

THE GULF STATES OF MEXICO

THE STATES OF NORTHERN MEXICO

THE PACIFIC SOUTH STATES OF MEXICO

THE STATES OF CENTRAL MEXICO

THE PACIFIC NORTH STATES OF MEXICO

MEXICO: FACTS AND FIGURES

INTRODUCTION

Mexico is a country in the midst of great change. And what happens in Mexico reverberates in the United States, its neighbor to the north.

For outsiders, the most obvious of Mexico's recent changes has occurred in the political realm. From 1929 until the end of the 20th century, the country was ruled by a single political party: the Partido Revolucionario Institucional, or PRI (in English, the Institutional Revolutionary Party). Over the years, PRI governments became notorious for corruption, and the Mexican economy languished. In 2000, however, the PRI's stranglehold on national politics was broken with the election of Vicente Fox as Mexico's president. Fox, of the Partido de Acción Nacional (National Action Party), or PAN, promised political reform and economic development but had a mixed record as president. However, another PAN candidate, Felipe Calderón, succeeded Fox in 2006 after a hotly contested and highly controversial election. That election saw Calderón win by the slimmest of margins over a candidate from the Partido de la Revolución Democrática (Party of the Democratic Revolution). The days of one-party rule in Mexico, it seems, are gone for good.

Mexico's economy, like its politics, has seen significant changes in recent years. A 1994 free-trade agreement with the United States and Canada, along with the increasing transfer of industries from government control to private ownership under President Fox and President Calderón, has helped spur economic growth in Mexico. When all the world's countries are compared,

Mexico now falls into the upper-middle range in per-capita income. This means that, on average, Mexicans enjoy a higher standard of living than people in the majority of the world's countries. Yet averages can be misleading. In Mexico there is an enormous gap between haves and have-nots. According to some estimates, 40 percent of the country's more than 100 million people live in poverty. In some areas of Mexico, particularly in rural villages, jobs are almost nonexistent. This has driven millions of Mexicans to immigrate to the United States (with or without proper documentation) in search of a better life.

By 2006 more than 11 million people born in Mexico were living in the United States (including more than 6 million illegal immigrants), according to estimates based on data from the Pew Hispanic Center and the U.S. Census Bureau. Meanwhile, nearly one of every 10 people living in the United States was of Mexican ancestry. Clearly, Mexico and Mexicans have had—and will continue to have—a major influence on American society.

It is especially unfortunate, then, that many American students know little about their country's neighbor to the south. The books in the MEXICO: BEAUTIFUL LAND, DIVERSE PEOPLE series are designed to help correct that.

As readers will discover, Mexico boasts a rich, vibrant culture that is a blend of indigenous and European—especially Spanish—influences. More than 3,000 years ago, the Olmec people created a complex society and built imposing monuments that survive to this day in the Mexican states of Tabasco and Veracruz. In the fifth century A.D., when the Roman Empire collapsed and Europe entered its so-called Dark Age, the Mayan civilization was already flourishing in the jungles of the Yucatán Peninsula—and it would enjoy another four centuries of tremendous cultural achievements. By the time the Spanish conqueror Hernán Cortés landed at Veracruz in 1519, another great indigenous civilization, the Aztecs, had emerged to dominate much of Mexico.

With a force of about 500 soldiers, plus a few horses and cannons, Cortés marched inland toward the Aztec capital, Tenochtitlán. Built in the middle of a lake in what is now Mexico City, Tenochtitlán was an engineering marvel and one of the largest cities anywhere in the world at the time. With allies from among the indigenous peoples who resented being ruled by the Aztecs—and aided by a smallpox epidemic—Cortés and the Spaniards managed to conquer the Aztec Empire in 1521 after a brutal fight that devastated Tenochtitlán.

It was in that destruction that modern Mexico was born. Spaniards married indigenous people, creating mestizo offspring—as well as a distinctive Mexican culture that was neither Spanish nor indigenous but combined elements of both.

Spain ruled Mexico for three centuries. After an unsuccessful revolution in 1810, Mexico finally won its independence in 1821.

But the newly born country continued to face many difficulties. Among them were bad rulers, beginning with a military officer named Agustín Iturbide, who had himself crowned emperor only a year after Mexico threw off the yoke of Spain. In 1848 Mexico lost a war with the United States—and was forced to give up almost half of its territory as a result. During the 1860s French forces invaded Mexico and installed a puppet emperor. While Mexico regained its independence in 1867 under national hero Benito Juárez, the long dictatorship of Porfirio Díaz would soon follow.

Díaz was overthrown in a revolution that began in 1910, but Mexico would be racked by fighting until the Partido Revolucionario Institucional took over in 1929. The PRI brought stability and economic progress, but its rule became increasingly corrupt.

Today, with the PRI's long monopoly on power swept away, Mexico stands on the brink of a new era. Difficult problems such as entrenched inequalities and grinding poverty remain. But progress toward a more open political system may lead to economic and social progress as well. Mexico—a land with a rich and ancient heritage—may emerge as one of the 21st century's most inspiring success stories.

The Pyramid of the Sun was built by the Mayans in the ancient city of Teotihuacán. Though it was constructed over a thousand years ago, it still stands today as a reminder of Mexico's unique history.

ARCHITECTURE

Architecture, the art or science of building, has a long history in Mexico that began with the civilizations who lived in this land long before the Spaniards came. The architecture of these ancient societies—the Olmecs, the Mayans, and the Aztecs—influenced today's Mexican buildings.

The culture of the Olmecs was one of the oldest, dating from around 1150 to 400 B.C. Although the Olmecs left no evidence that they built any great cities, they did leave the remains of their ceremonial centers. Archeologists now believe that these were lively settlements where artists, farmers, priests, and rulers once lived. One important feature of these centers was their system of stone *aqueducts* that provided drinking water to the various areas of each settlement.

Another very important architectural structure in this *pre-Hispanic* period was the pyramid. The Olmecs built pyramids in the shape of volcanoes, perhaps imitating the two huge volcanoes that overshadowed central Mexico. Although no one is certain what these pyramids were used for, they were usually part of a *complex* of buildings used for religious ceremonies.

At one Olmec site called La Venta stands a pyramid built of packed clay over 100 feet tall. Pillars of basalt (a very dark, hard rock) surround the pyramid, and the basalt was apparently dug out of the ground over 60 miles away. Archeologists have not been able to solve the mystery of how the heavy rock was carried such a long distance. At La Venta, archeologists also found the remains of a ball court, where games using rubber balls were once played. Other structures that have given archeologists clues to the Olmec culture are enormous stone altars covered with carvings.

Around A.D. 300, some time after the Olmecs, the culture of the Maya emerged on the Yucatán Peninsula. Like the Olmecs' architecture, the great structures of the Maya were stages set for their ceremonial culture. The buildings for everyday use, built of reeds, mud, and wood, have not survived, while the beautiful cities where religious and political ceremonies took place still stand. The buildings in these complexes included limestone ball courts, gateways, *plazas*, and water reservoirs.

Although the Maya built pyramids like the Olmecs, the Mayan structures were even more impressive. The Mayan pyramids were built of rubble but covered with smooth limestone. These tall structures were considered to be holy places, for they linked the earth and the heavens. Some had dramatic steps that climbed the front of the pyramids to temples on top. Others were burial chambers for royalty.

The culture of the Maya was very sophisticated, and they built more complicated structures than other ancient Mexican cultures. For example, the *corbel*

The enormous Pyramid of the Sun was 700 feet square and 217 feet high.

12

Early Mexican cultures showed appreciation to their gods by creating on a grand scale. This giant head made by the Olmecs was found among the ruins of La Venta, an important ceremonial center.

vault found in Mayan architecture is the only example of an *arch* found in pre-Hispanic buildings. The Maya needed to understand complex math to figure out how to build the arch so it would not collapse.

Separated from Mayan territory by jungle and mountains was another culture of great builders. The ruins of the city of Teotihuacán, built by the dominant culture of central Mexico around A.D. 150, stand near present-day Mexico City. It was a carefully planned city, set up on a *grid* pattern and divided into four parts. There were multi-family apartment complexes, elaborate palaces, temples, courtyards, and ball courts. This very ancient civilization was probably first established a hundred years after the birth of Christ, and it collapsed around A.D. 750.

The most awesome structures of Teotihuacán are the Pyramids of the Sun and Moon. These pyramids are centered on the Avenue of the

Christianity figures prominently in the lives of many Mexicans. This cathedral, built in Mexico City over a century ago, remains a vital part of the city and of Mexican culture.

Dead, a great boulevard nearly a mile long and very wide. The pyramids were made of earth, *adobe* bricks, and rubble, then faced with stone, covered with plaster, and painted.

The ruins of Teotihuacán influenced the architecture of the Aztecs, the last great civilization of the pre-Hispanic period. The Aztecs included several cultures who spoke the same language and lived in central Mexico at the time of the Spanish *conquest*. The strongest group was the Mexica Aztecs, who build the great city of Tenochtitlán.

The builders of Tenochtitlán mixed the architecture of previous cultures. They borrowed ideas, such as the careful urban planning of Teotihuacán. Buildings for grain and *arsenals* of weapons were placed

The Baroque cathedrals had two distinguishing features: The cupola was a cylindrical vault, which formed part of the ceiling. The azulejo was the colorful tile used on cupolas and roofs.

strategically throughout the city. Botanical gardens grew among the buildings, and beautiful tall palaces, the homes of nobles, stood in the center of the city. Like the Olmecs and the Mayans, the Aztecs built pyramids. At the top were temples to their gods, Tlaloc (the rain god) and Huitzilopochtli (the war god).

When the Spanish came to Mexico in the 16th century, they were deeply impressed by the city of Tenochtitlán. The streets were wide and straight, the buildings tall and beautiful, and somewhere between 150,000 and 300,000 people lived there. This meant it was one of the largest cities in the world at that time. However, the Spaniards were horrified by the Aztecs' practice of human sacrifice. The Spanish leaders decided they would destroy the Aztecs' temples and altars, and they built their own structures on the ruins. Tenochtitlán's ruins still lie beneath today's Mexico City.

Beginning with the Spaniards' conquest, the colonial period of architecture lasted for more than 200 years and spanned a huge range of styles. From the fortress-like buildings of the Conquest period to the *Baroque* and the *Neoclassical* periods, colonial architecture in Mexico mirrored the changes in European styles of building.

At first, the most important buildings were churches. Over 13,000 were built during the colonial period. The earliest permanent structures, these churches were built on the ruins of Indian cities by Indian workers and stonemasons, as the Spanish focused on converting the native Mexicans to Christianity. Built like some *medieval* churches in Europe, the fortress church

Neoclassical means a revival of the simple, stately architecture of ancient Greece and Rome.

had two towers and a courtyard surrounded by walls with *parapets* on top. Unlike European churches, the walls of Mexican churches were extremely thick, in order to defend against Indian attacks and withstand earthquakes.

In the 17th and early 18th centuries, Spanish rule in Mexico became more stable, and the colonial settlers became wealthier. As a result, the latest European style, Baroque architecture, flourished. This style was rich and sumptuous. In Mexico, the Baroque builders blended Spanish and native styles. Baroque *cathedrals* were massive structures, requiring many years of labor. For example, the huge cathedral in Morelia was begun in 1690 and completed in 1740. The Baroque cathedral in Mexico City, one of the most lavish in the world, took over 250 years to complete.

As the colonial people of Mexico grew more prosperous, the architecture grew more elaborate, with fanciful carving and sculpture decorating every surface area in some churches. This late Mexican Baroque style was called the Churrigueresque style. Much of the elaborate detail and design was unique to Mexican architecture. It demonstrated the influence of native artisans who continued to use their own traditions for decoration.

By the late 18th century, European taste reacted against the overly fancy Baroque style, and colonial Mexico imitated the new style, Neoclassical architecture. Many *civic* buildings and some churches were built in this style, which was more influenced by the culture of France than Spain. The style's simple formality didn't allow for the influence of native Mexican culture. The famous Mexican art school, the Academy of San Carlos, was built in this style.

The remains of Mayan temples and ceremonial centers still dot the Mexican landscape. The ruins in Quintana Roo overlook the Mexican coastline.

The colonial era in Mexico ended with the War of Independence, which began in 1810. Even though independence inspired a celebration of Mexican culture, not much building took place during the period of upheaval that followed the war. As a result, there is no particular architectural style that marks this period.

However, when Porfirio Díaz took control of the presidency in 1876, he brought more than 30 years of relative peace and prosperity for the upper class of Mexican society. This created a period of urban building. During this era, often called the Porfiriato, most architecture was influenced by European styles. Buildings imitated Parisian stately homes, Italian-style details decorated government offices, and Victorian influences appeared across Mexico City in the lacy *cast iron* that ornamented many homes.

After the Mexican Revolution, which began in 1910, Mexican artists and intellectuals wanted to celebrate their culture's exciting blend of

The Mayans were one of the most powerful civilizations of the ancient world. Their architecture, in turn, influenced the Aztecs, the last great native civilization of ancient Mexico.

native and Spanish influences. The modern period of architecture was affected by this enthusiasm for a uniquely Mexican culture, yet it was also influenced by European radical architectural ideas.

A very important architect in this period, Juan O'Gorman (1905–1982), was not only an architect but also a painter, *muralist*, and mosaicist (which means he made *mosaics* of brightly colored tile). O'Gorman traveled in Europe and brought what was called the International Style back to Mexico.

This style of architecture chose simple shapes over complex designs. Architects were concerned with the function of buildings and used modern materials, like steel and concrete. O'Gorman was interested in both modern French architecture and pre-Hispanic Mexican structures, such as pyramids. Both influences shaped his buildings, and he designed many schools for the Mexican government in this style.

In the 1950s, O'Gorman became interested in mosaics. He incorporated patterns from pre-Hispanic culture into his designs. His best-known mosaic covers four sides of the Central Library at the National Autonomous University, which he designed.

Contemporary architects have followed in the footsteps of O'Gorman. Félix Candela was known for designing thin-shelled domes for stadiums. Pedro Ramírez Vásquez, who designed the National Museum of Anthropology, also combined modern international ideas with an interest in the forms and patterns of Mexico's most ancient structures.

The influence of long-ago cultures can still be seen in today's Mexican architecture. As we shall see, these ancient people also left their mark on other aspects of Mexico's arts.

19

The capital of Mexico, Mexico City, has long been an intellectual and artistic center. This mosaic, created by Mexican artist Diego Rivera, illustrates many important events of Mexico's history in the vibrant, colorful style commonly attached to the country's art.

THE VISUAL ARTS:
PAINTING AND SCULPTURE

Pre-Hispanic Mexican art is a record of ancient ideas about beauty and power. We find this record not only in painting and sculpture but also in these cultures' writing systems, which were based on images. The art of these various civilizations tended to tell a story that was filled with images of people.

Olmec artists carved sculptures of strong male bodies, showing political or supernatural power. The most striking sculptures that have survived the centuries are enormous stone heads, made of **basalt**. As much as nine feet tall and weighing several tons, these impressive works of art were possibly portraits of Olmec leaders. The faces look very natural, with fleshy cheeks and lips, and most heads are wearing helmets (perhaps worn during ceremonial ball games).

The Maya also loved to portray the human body in their many paintings and sculptures. Their beautiful images of men and women were sometimes clearly portraits of specific persons. The Maya created artwork everywhere. They decorated many of their buildings with stone or plaster carvings. Their murals, painted skillfully in vivid colors, show what life was like in the Maya's day. For example, at Bonampak (a Mayan site in southern Mexico), painted rooms portray the cycle of Mayan kingship.

In contrast, at Teotihuacán, artists used patterns and designs more than images of people in their painting and sculpture. The images of human forms that do exist seem more like designs than portraits of individuals. For example, in the temple complex, the sculptures of gods have human forms, but they have expressionless faces and stiff, rectangular bodies.

The last pre-Hispanic culture, the Aztecs, borrowed ideas for sculpture and painting from the past. In Tenochtitlán, sculpture often decorated buildings. The temple complex contained frightening carvings of gods and figures from myths, but there were also some beautiful, non-threatening sculptures of animals and past Aztec rulers.

After the Spaniards' arrival in Mexico, colonial art included styles from four major European periods: medieval, Renaissance, Baroque, and Neoclassical. The earliest art, shaped by European medieval styles, were church statues and decorative stonework. Created by Indian artisans, these carvings often mixed Indian designs with images of Catholic saints.

Later, the inside walls of churches and monasteries were covered with paintings, like the churches in

Retablos were carved altars, an important part of colonial sculpture, which could be made of wood or plaster. A great Baroque retablo is in Mexico City, at the cathedral. This huge altar, carved in wood in 1724 by Spanish sculptor Jerónimo de Balbás, is covered with gold leaf, with elaborately carved columns and painted statues.

Two of the greatest artists in modern Mexican history were Frida Kahlo and Diego Rivera, who were twice married. Their opinions and feelings about Mexico were often reflected in their paintings, whether murals or self-portraits.

24

Renaissance Europe. Some work was done by Spanish artists, but Indian artists often painted these murals. Most painting from this time was religious, filled with images of angels and saints. It was art with a message, intending to teach the common people about Christianity.

In the Baroque period, individual Mexican artists began to distinguish themselves. For example, Juan Correa (1680–1715) was an important painter of the 18th century known for his original Mexican style. Correa blended the European realistic style of painting with a native drawing style. Because he used local people as models, his images of saints looked Mexican. He was so successful that he even had paintings hung in the Cathedral in Mexico City, including his masterpiece, *The Assumption of the Virgin*.

Sculpture was important during the Baroque period. The 17th-century Mexican masters were Tomás Xuárez and his son, Salvador de Ocampo. Their woodcarving combined Baroque decoration with carefully carved biblical

Diego Rivera was a passionate and intense artist, and a great deal of his works concern the Mexican Revolution as well as the Mexican national identity. Many of his murals can still be seen on buildings, both inside and out, in Mexico.

scenes. Known for their carved *retablos*, this father and son adapted European-style sculpture to their Mexican roots.

During the 18th century, Mexican art's focus shifted away from religious art as Neoclassicism influenced sculpture and painting. An important figure in this period was Manuel Tolsá (1757–1816), a sculptor and architect, who was born in Spain but was a very influential teacher at the Mexican art school, the San Carlos Academy. He taught his students to draw from the plaster casts of ancient Roman and Greek statues he had brought with him from Spain. His calm and formal Neoclassical style can be seen in his famous bronze sculpture of King Charles IV of Spain, which still stands in Mexico City.

Even after Mexican Independence from Spain, Mexican artists, many of whom were taught by Spanish teachers at the San Carlos Academy, continued to follow European styles. Felipe Gutiérrez (1824–1904) skillfully painted *Saint Jerome* and *Saint Bartholomew* in warm colors with natural expressions. Other artists tried to give their work Mexican subjects but were hampered by the European style they had been taught. For instance, José Obrégon (1832–1902) painted *The Discovery of Pulque*; although the setting of the painting is pre-Hispanic Mexico, the scenery looks European.

The 19th century saw other visual art forms flourish. Discontent with Porfirio Díaz's political power inspired the humorous prints of José Guadalupe Posada (1852–1913). He was a graphic artist in Mexico City, who published his prints in

Pulque was an alcoholic drink made by the Aztecs and drunk in Mexico to this day. It's made from the maguey (agave) plant, a succulent cactus with spiny leaves.

periodicals. He was famous for prints of skulls, which made fun of Mexican middle-class society, and his illustrations of sensational events, such as murders, accidents, and scandals. Posada's art was a form of political and social criticism. Because he used his drawings to express ideas and emotions, he wasn't held back by the formal rules taught at the art schools. Popular art, like Posada's prints, was often more inventive and livelier than that created by the art schools.

By the end of the 19th century, even some academic painters began to break away from European rules and styles of art. José María Velasco (1840–1902) is considered Mexico's best 19th-century painter. He had a fine sense of color and was good at creating large compositions. A geologist and **botanist**, Velasco was interested in how the Mexican landscape connected with Mexican history. His most famous works use the Valley of Mexico as its subject.

A turn-of-the-century painter who also looked at his native land of Mexico for inspiration was Saturnino Herrán (1887–1918). A great draftsman and painter, his paintings are about the people of Mexico. His best-known painting, *The Offering*, is filled with warm colors and a peaceful composition, treating the Mexican tradition it portrays with respect and sadness.

Most murals were frescoes. Fresco painting is a very old technique of applying oil paint directly onto the wet plaster of a wall. The painting then becomes a durable, lasting part of the structure of the building on which it was painted.

After the Revolution of 1910, the Mexican art world exploded into life. The Revolution celebrated Mexico's pre-Hispanic past, allowing artists to break away from European traditions. Murals, large works

Rufino Tamayo was an artist who did not try to make a political statement with his artwork. Unlike many other popular artists of his time, his paintings were deeply personal rather than historical.

painted directly onto walls, were the most important art form at this time.

An important figure in this artistic revolution was Dr. Atl (Gerardo Murillo), a teacher at the San Carlos Academy who wanted to revive mural art in Mexico. He said that art should be for the people. Another important figure was José Vasconcelos, the Minister of Education, who persuaded the government to pay muralists to paint public buildings. However, the most important people in the artistic revolution were three muralists, known as "The Big Three": Diego Rivera, David Alfaro Siqueiros, and José Clemente Orozco.

Diego Rivera (1886–1957) is probably the most famous of these artists. As a student at the San Carlos Academy, he took classes with José María Velasco and Dr. Atl—but he also visited the print shop where Posada worked. He studied in Europe for nearly 15 years, learning from

The library at the University of Mexico is completely covered with traditional Mexican symbols and images. The building in Mexico City is evidence of Mexico's great national pride.

both the great Spanish Renaissance paintings and the modern styles of French artists like Picasso and Matisse. Perhaps, however, the Renaissance *frescoes* in Italian churches most influenced his work. When he returned to Mexico, he visited the Mayan ruins in the Yucatán, which reinforced his belief that everything of value in Mexico has Indian roots.

His first big project, the murals on the walls of the Secretariat of Public Education, combined what he had learned in Europe with his feelings about the native roots of Mexican art. An enormous project, he painted over 100 murals on walls three stories high and a city block long. It took him more than three years to complete. In these huge murals, Rivera wanted to show the negative and positive aspects of Mexican culture. From his perspective, institutions like the Church, the military, and industry were bad for Mexican culture, while the people of Mexico, the workers, *peasants*, and soldiers, made Mexican culture great. Critics consider Rivera's best murals to be the ones he painted at the National Agricultural School at Chapingo. However, Rivera stirred up controversy in both his work and personal life. He was married four times, twice to fellow-artist Frida Kahlo. Also, he was dismissed from his association with the Mexican Marxists for accepting too many jobs from rich patrons. One of Rivera's last murals, *Dream of a Sunday Afternoon in the Alameda*, painted in Mexico City's Prado Hotel, created a huge controversy because he wrote, "There is no God" (in Spanish), on the mural. He later removed the phrase, so that the mural could be enjoyed by the public for whom he painted it.

The second important muralist, David Alfaro Siqueiros (1896–1974), was an equally controversial figure. A committed Marxist and labor organizer, Siqueiros went to prison several times. His work was dramatic and full of non-traditional ideas. Unlike Rivera, he was not fascinated by native Mexican themes. Instead,

Marxists believed the political theories of Karl Marx, a German philosopher of the 19th century. Many Mexican artists were Marxists after the Revolution, because Marxist ideas supported their beliefs that art should serve the common people and not be something for the rich to buy and collect.

he was much more interested in the struggle of urban workers. He experimented with spray guns to apply paint, and he used acrylic paints rather than oils.

The final figure in the "Big Three" was José Clemente Orozco (1883–1949), a less-flamboyant artist than either Rivera or Siqueiros. Like Rivera, he was influenced by both Posada's and Dr. Atl's ideas about the purposes of art, and his paintings were a form of social criticism. In compositions full of movement and rich colors, he painted the seedy side of urban life and the horrors of war, which he had seen firsthand as a soldier in the Revolution.

Although mural painting was the most important aspect of Mexican art until the 1940s, the vibrant artistic atmosphere influenced other kinds of painting as well. Frida Kahlo (1907–1954) was a painter who received attention for her primitivist style, Marxism, and interest in Mexican identity. Her art was more personal than that of the muralists. In her paintings, she explored her relationship to Rivera and her lifelong pain as a result of a terrible traffic accident. However, like Rivera, her identity as a Mexican was essential to her work.

Kahlo's health caused her much suffering throughout her adult life, but she never gave up on her art. Eventually, she had to have her legs amputated below the knee. Rather than feel sorry for herself, she wrote in her journal: "Feet, what do I need them for when I have wings to fly?"

Art critics have observed that the style of her work was like that of the surrealists. Surrealist painters used symbols and strange combinations of objects to explore dream-like states of mind. Kahlo also imitated "primitive" painters, untrained artists who ignored the rules for painting objects realistically. As a result, Kahlo's paintings are colorful and mysterious, innocent-looking, but full of hidden meanings.

Rufino Tamayo (1899–1991) is another painter, muralist, and sculptor whose work had a big impact on Mexican painting. Unlike the "Big Three," he didn't think art was supposed to have a political message. Tamayo's work used intense color and semi-*abstract* images, but his paintings were much more personal.

Born in Oaxaca of Zapotec Indian parents, Tamayo studied pre-Hispanic art when he worked for the National Museum of Anthropology. Pre-Hispanic forms, themes, and colors shaped his work, but Tamayo also lived in Europe and New York. This international influence allowed his work to become even more abstract and personal in the 1950s.

Tamayo's work influenced many contemporary Mexican artists, for example, José Luis Cuevas (1934–   ), who works in paint and printmaking. Cuevas' work is often about loneliness and isolation, and he paints the poorest people of Mexico City. Another contemporary artist influenced by Tamayo is Francisco Toledo (1941–   ), who is a printmaker, sculptor, painter, and photographer. His work reveals his interest in the religion and history of ancient Mexico.

The changes in Mexican art that began after the Revolution lasted for many years, up to the present day. The influence of ancient pre-Hispanic art has endured even longer. Mexican visual arts reflect the nation's history, creating a powerful art style like none other.

Bullfighting is considered more than a sport in Mexico; some view it as an art. Both the rituals inherent in the fight and the ornate costumes worn by the bullfighters are carefully planned for maximum impact.

THE PERFORMING ARTS:

MUSIC, DANCE, AND THEATER

Public performances played a huge role in the lives of pre-Hispanic Mexicans. However, these performances did not simply entertain the audience. Many were rituals, which portrayed myths and beliefs. Temples were ritual theaters, where humans acted out the roles of gods, animal spirits, and ancestors.

The archeological record gives an incomplete account of these performances. No one knows what they sounded like or how they were staged. Objects these cultures left behind give partial clues, however. For example, Olmec rituals probably used the masks, some beautiful and some terrifying, that have been found at Olmec sites.

Music, song, and dance flourished during the pre-Hispanic period. Carvings and murals show that musical instruments included ceramic flutes, gourd rattles, drums, trumpets made of wood or conch shells, reed whistles, and notch-stick rasps. This visual record also shows ancient people performing dances, some of which continue to be performed by native Mexicans to this day. Ancient dances include the *Danza de los Voladores* (Dance of the Fliers), in which dancers hanging from ropes fly around a pole 100 feet high.

Musical and dance performances were an important part of Aztec ceremonies of religion and government. Some dances were sacred, such as the dance performed when praying to the rain god, Tlaloc. Music and song also helped poets remember and recite long oral histories and poetry. The Nahuatl language of the Aztecs lacks any distinction between poem and song, and their poetry was sung, not just spoken.

After Spain conquered Mexico, however, most music came from Spain. The sacred music of the Catholic Church, with its choirs and organs, largely silenced native song, but some native styles were adapted for religious purposes. Popular music and dances also came from Spain, such as *sones, fandangos, tiranas,* and *boleros*. These songs were played on the Spanish guitar, which became a popular instrument with the common people and with the settlers who couldn't bring heavier or more delicate instruments with them on their journeys.

For those who lived in Mexico City and other urban areas, performances imitated those of Europe. Many wealthy Mexicans of the colonial era enjoyed attending

Many ancient Mexican cultures had a ball game ritual. Players enacted a myth about a struggle between gods through the competition of the game. They had to get a rubber ball through a stone hoop on the side of the ball court, but they could only touch the ball with their hips, elbows, and knees. The loser of the game would be sacrificed. This ball game could substitute for actual battle between cities.

Mariachi bands perform the distinct music of Mexico for natives and tourists alike. Mexico's culture comes alive through the performance of traditional music and dance.

the opera, and most operas performed in Mexico were written by European composers. However, the first Mexican opera, *La Púrpera de la rosa (The Blood of the Rose)*, was performed in 1701.

Mexican theater followed European models as well. Common people enjoyed morality plays performed in churches, while secular theaters, often beautiful, grand buildings, provided a place for wealthy Mexicans to enjoy popular dramas from France and Spain.

After Independence and during the Porfiriato, the conditions for

The Ballet Folklórico de México interprets and retells the history of Mexico through its unique style of dance. The dance troupe, founded by Amalia Hernández in 1952, expresses the drama and passion of Mexico's people.

Mexican performing arts changed a little. On the one hand, the influence of European styles of music, dance, and drama dominated the cultural life of Mexico. Many large, European-style theaters were built, such as the Teatro Degollado in Guadalajara and the Gran Teatro (finished in 1843) in Mexico City, which was built for opera, ballet, and symphonic music. On the other hand, however, a period called the *Renaciamento* (Rebirth) began after the war for independence. During this time of new life, artists felt proud of their Mexican identity. They took up Mexican themes in their work, and this produced some Italian-style operas that incorporated native Mexican themes and musical patterns. For example, Melesio Morales

(1838–1908) composed the opera *Anita*, which was set in Mexico during the War of Independence. Even more Mexican was the work of Aniceto Ortega (1823-1875), who composed the opera *Guatemotzin* about the struggle between the Aztecs and Spaniards for control of Mexico. This was the first effort by a Mexican composer to incorporate elements of pre-Hispanic music.

In spite of these works, however, upper-class Mexicans preferred the music of European composers and their Mexican imitators. Even Juventino Rosas, an Otami Indian, did not write music in a style that would be considered Mexican but instead composed European-style music, including a famous set of waltzes.

As with other aspects of Mexican art, the Revolution greatly changed attitudes in the performing arts. Composers and **choreographers** became much more interested in creating works that reflected the history and heritage of their native Mexico.

One composer of this era was Manual Ponce (1882–1948). Ponce spent his early career conducting, teaching, and composing. After studying in Paris in the 1920s, he changed his style. When he returned to Mexico, he composed a symphonic poem called *Chapultepec* using elements of Mexican folk music. He even chose to compose for an instrument that was historically important in Mexico, the guitar. His compositions for guitar are his best-known work today.

Another Mexican composer, one of the most famous of this time, was Carlos Chávez (1899–1978). He

Morality plays came from Europe in the Middle Ages. These plays taught a moral lesson; they were about characters that represented an abstract quality—such as faith, hope, or charity.

The performing arts of music and dance have existed in Mexico since ancient times, as evidenced by this Mayan carving. The rock, found in Oaxaca, shows a man performing a ritual dance.

studied with Ponce early in his career, after Ponce developed his interest in native music. Chávez won praise for his "Sinfonía India" and "El Sol," compositions that both had strong rhythm, clear melody, and used the percussion style of native Mexican music. His interest in native music also influenced other Mexican composers. Chávez's other accomplishments include founding the *Orquesta Sinfónica de México* (Mexican Symphony), composing music for ballets, and writing two operas, as well as being a music critic.

Popular music experienced a revival during this era, especially *mariachi* music, which originated in the string bands of rural

Michoácan. Originally, the mariachi bands' instruments included guitar, *vihuela* (a small five-string guitar), one or two violins, and a harp or *guitarrón* (a large bass guitar). In the 1930s, with the new technologies of radio and film, mariachi music became very popular, and the now-familiar trumpets were added to the bands.

In recent times, one of the great developments in Mexican performing arts was the founding of the Ballet Folklórico de México by Amalia Hernández (1917–2000). A choreographer, prima ballerina, and director, Hernández founded this dance troupe in 1952. Her goal was to revive the traditions of Mexico and present their complexity and beauty to the world. As a choreographer, she drew on the great variety of Mexican dances, some derived from Aztec and Mayan traditions, others from popular village *fiesta* traditions. Her dancers transformed regional folk dances into stylized theatrical performances. Describing her work, Hernández explained: "I try to go to the most profound roots of folklore and tradition, but my intention is to create a show—a show with Mexican sources and Mexican blood."

Although theater and drama lagged behind the other performing arts in finding its Mexican identity, these art forms have seen recent growth. For example, Vicente Leñero's play, *Nadie Sabe Nada*, was a much-praised parody of Mexican politics. The play was so controversial in 1988 that government *censors* shut it down, but it reopened when Lenero agreed to delete the offensive section.

Today, in a more tolerant atmosphere, dramatists have had more opportunity to explore political issues. Mexican performing arts continue to be a powerful expression of this nation's history and culture.

Octavio Paz was one of the most acclaimed writers and poets in contemporary Mexico. He received the Nobel Prize for literature in 1990, solidifying international respect for his work.

THE LITERARY ARTS

Mexican literature has a history that reaches back nearly 2,000 years. Not only did pre-Hispanic Mexican culture have an oral tradition of songs and poems, but they also had the means to write and record their literature.

The Mayan writing system had over 400 hieroglyphs, representing numbers, dates, colors, and abstract ideas. Recordings were made in stone, pottery, and paper made from tree bark.

The various Aztec tribes also had a rich literary tradition. Written in the Nahuatl language, their literature contained mythic stories and poetry, including a *flor y cantos* (flower and song) tradition. These poems sometimes were connected to rituals like harvest ceremonies, but many poems were written simply for literary pleasure, not just religious or historical purposes. For example, 30 ancient poems by Nezahualcoyotl of Texcoco, the philosopher king, have been preserved; many of these describe how quickly life passes. Besides poetry, Aztec literature included history and philosophical treatises recorded on paper made from bark.

During the colonial period, much writing was about Spanish

exploration. The Spanish were interested in converting the native Mexicans to Christianity, so many priests wrote down what they had learned about native cultures, especially the religious practices. When Spanish rule was secure, other kinds of writing began to appear in Mexico.

One of the most gifted writers of this era was Sor Juana Inéz de la Cruz (1651–1695), a poet, scholar, and nun. A child who was mature for her age, she wrote her first poem at the age of eight. As a teenager, she decided to join the Convent of St. Jerome in order to devote herself to an intellectual life. She explained this choice in her later writings, saying that a writer's life would have been impossible for a married woman. Sor Juana wrote plays, essays, and poetry about the position and treatment of women. Her work was funny and passionate.

One of Sor Juana's friends was Carlos de Sigüenza y Góngora (1645–1700), an intellectual priest who wrote poetry, mostly on the religious topics typical of that era. His best-known work is a poem about the Virgin of Guadalupe.

Another poet-priest was Bernardo de Balbuena (1561–1627). He wrote a long lyrical poem called *Grandeza Mexica* (1603) that praised the beauty of Mexico City, its women, theaters, and intellectuals.

During the years of the struggle for independence, the leading literary figure was José Joaquín Fernández de

The *Popul Vuh* is an important Mayan work of literature, because it tells the story of the mythological origins of the Mayan people. After the Spanish conquest, a native Mayan used his own language and Spanish script to record this part of Mayan mythology. Another Mayan work was the *Libros de Chilam Balam*, a book about the Mayan vision of history.

Carlos Fuentes is one of the best-known Mexican novelists in the world today. Like many contemporary writers in Mexico, his books address social and political concerns.

Lizardi (1776–1827), who was a novelist, journalist, and political activist. When the struggle for independence began, he founded a newspaper called *El Pensador Mexicano (The Mexican Thinker)*. Believing that reading and writing were important to changing Mexico into an independent republic, he created the Public Society of Reading in 1820, which distributed books and newspapers. While he was imprisoned for writing about his views, he wrote what is considered Mexico's first novel, whose title is translated as *The Itching Parrot* (1816).

After the War for Independence and the War of Reform, the

Sor Juana Inéz de la Cruz is one of the most recognized historical figures in Mexico. Her striking literary assertions about gender roles and misconceptions are as pointed and challenging today as they were in the 17th century.

movement called the *Renaciamento* (Rebirth) began, which tried to use literature, art, and education to build a national identity. This influenced Mexican novels the most. For example, Manuel Ignacio Altamirano, an Indian novelist and critic, urged writers to break away from the French style. Instead, he said that writers should develop the Mexican novel by writing about Mexican themes. One of his most famous novels, *El Zarco*, was an adventure story about highway bandits.

Another popular novel of this period was about specifically Mexican characters. *Astucia, jefe de los hermanos de la boja, (Astucia, Chief of the Woodsmen)*, written in an informal style by Luis G. Inclán, is the story of men of action who were suspicious of politicians. Unlike European-style novels, the characters spoke in the plain Spanish of Mexican ranchers.

During the Porfiriato, European culture again became important, although the middle-class reading public still wanted novels about Mexican subjects. A poet from this period is Manuel Gutiérrez Nájera (1859–1895), whose work was clearly influenced by Europe. Important to Mexican Modernism, he tried to give new life to the language of Spanish poetry. Like the modern French poetry he imitated, his work was elegant and somber. Nájera was considered one of the best of Mexico's poets, even though he was criticized for not caring how his art affected society.

After the Revolution, writers were encouraged to portray realistically the lives of the Mexican people. One of these writers was Mariano Azuela (1873–1952), a novelist who wrote about the Revolution. Born in Jalisco, Azuela was a doctor who served with Pancho Villa in the Revolution. He wrote *Los de abajo* (*The Underdogs*, 1916) while serving as an army doctor. Instead of praising the Revolution, this

This poem, written by Acoyuan, an Aztec poet (c. 1490) is a good example of the *flor y cantos* tradition:

Will I have to go like the flowers that perish?
Will nothing remain of my name?
Nothing of my fame here on earth?
At least my flowers, at least my songs!
Earth is the region of the fleeting moment.
Is it also thus in the place
Where in some way one lives?
Is there joy there, is there friendship?
Or is it only here on earth
We come to know our faces?

novel criticized the revolutionaries for abusing the power they had seized, and it described how idealists usually got killed, letting the opportunists take over. The protagonist, Demetrio Macías, leader of a group of Indians, becomes a general under Villa. Caught up the turmoil of the Revolution, Macías lacks good judgment and doesn't know why he is fighting. Azuela believed this confusion was typical of the Mexican Revolution. Like other writers of his period, he wanted to write about reality, no matter how discouraging it was.

The contemporary period has been a great age for Mexican literature. Writers have produced work that challenges the imagination with its rich language. One of Mexico's greatest poets, Octavio Paz (1914–1998), won a Nobel Prize in 1990. Influenced by the French symbolists and Nájera, Paz's poems are difficult and full of allusions. His most famous book, *The Labyrinth of Solitude* (1950), was not poetry but a collection of essays; they explore the idea that Mexico has been haunted by its violent past and its history of betrayal by its leaders.

Another contemporary writer who developed the same theme was Juan Rulfo (1918–1986). He wrote two major works, *Pedro Páramo* (1955), a novel, and *El llano en llamas* (*The Burning Plain*, 1953), a collection of short stories. Both works focus on the poverty and despair in rural Mexico. Rulfo was a leader of a writing style called "magical realism." Works written in this style show everyday issues and normal details mixed with elements of magic or dreams.

Probably the best-known Mexican writer is Carlos Fuentes (1928-). His

The Virgin of Guadalupe is a very important figure in Mexican art. According to Catholic tradition, this vision of the Virgin Mary appeared to Juan Diego, an Aztec man, in 1531.

The Virgin Mary holds special religious meaning to devout Christian Mexicans. She is often called Our Lady of Guadalupe, because she appeared to a Mexican man in Guadalupe in 1531. During parades in her honor, the image of Mary is carried through the streets to the church built where she is believed to have appeared.

most famous novel, *La muerte de Artemio Cruz* (*The Death of Artemio Cruz*, 1962), is about an illegitimate boy who grew up to fight in the Revolution. He became corrupt, rich, and powerful, but he died a lonely old man. The story's point of view alternates between memories of the past and the deathbed of Cruz. Fuentes's skill in structuring this story shows why he has an international reputation as a great novelist.

From pre-Hispanic days until the present day, Mexican writers have produced works that merit a place in the world's great literature. Authors like Paz, Rulfo, and Fuentes prove that the Mexican creative heritage continues to build on its rich literary history.

FOLK ART

Mexican folk arts have their roots in the pre-Hispanic cultures of Mexico. However, these traditional art forms changed over time as they were influenced by outside cultures and the demands of the market.

Folk art is different from other forms of art because most folk art comes from the impulse to make everyday objects beautiful. Unlike other forms of art created by professional, trained artists, self-trained craftspeople make folk art. They mix creativity with practicality, and they are usually considered artisans, not artists.

When the Spanish arrived in Mexico, they found the origins of what is now called folk art: textiles of fine cotton; headdresses and cloaks made of feathers; jewelry and ritual objects made of silver, gold, and copper; and all sorts of other artistic handiwork, such as woodcarving, mosaics, and basketry. The Spanish introduced to the native artisans new materials, like wool, iron, and glass. The Spanish also brought new

Mexico's folk art tells of its history, traditions, and people. This papier-mâché "happy skeleton" was created for the celebration of the Day of the Dead, a festival held every November 2 to honor the deceased.

Dr. Atl (Geraldo Murillo, the man who started the revival of mural painting in Mexico) organized the first major show of native arts and crafts in 1921 as the director of the new government's Department of Fine Arts. Objects at the show included pottery, papier-mâché figures, ceramics, and lacquerwork.

techniques, including the potter's wheel, glazing for ceramics, and tooled leatherwork.

For the next three centuries, artisans sold their beautiful and useful works to others who used them for the purpose for which

The art of making pottery serves as a creative outlet for Mexicans. The pottery can be used for practical or decorative purposes, and can generate a profit in open-air markets or tourist shops.

they were created. But this changed after the Revolution. Because of more positive ways of thinking about Mexico's native past, a new interest in Mexican folk art was born. Mexican folk art was now sold on the tourist market, which was beginning to flourish in the 1920s. People began to collect and display folk art, rather than use it. These objects are as various as the materials available for turning ordinary objects into something beautiful.

For instance, woodcarving has thrived in Mexico. Artisans have made many beautiful religious objects, such as *retablos*, carved and painted altar frames, and *bultos*, which are carved images of saints. Mexican woodcarvers have also displayed their skills in the creation of furniture and wooden chests painted with unique designs.

Folk art and handcrafts such as weaving are an important part of Mexico's culture, and also bring in money from tourists, collectors, and enthusiasts. This Mexican marketplace boasts colorful serapes (shawl-like wraps), purses, and bags.

Mexican pottery, one of the most ancient forms of folk art, comes in a huge variety of styles and designs. Pre-Hispanic artisans created beautiful pottery without a potter's wheel, a specialized craft that was passed down from parents to children. And pottery continues to be very important in Mexico. Different regions specialize in different styles. For example, black pottery from Oaxaca is popular on the tourist market. In Puebla, artisans produce not just pottery but also tiles.

Metalwork is another important form of folk art. Prior to the Spanish conquest, natives used gold, silver, and copper only, but the Spanish introduced iron and tin, metals now used often in Mexican folk art. A colonial law kept natives from using precious metals, and as a result tin became an important material in Mexican craftwork. Native Mexicans who wanted to decorate their churches began a tradition of making tin candelabras, lamps, and sacred vessels.

Mexican textiles are crafted by hand for the purpose of beauty and function, most of which are worn as part of various tribal costumes. Certain pieces of clothing have traditionally been crafted with painstaking attention to detail. For example, *huipiles* are lavishly embroidered dresses (or blouses—they can reach to the waist or knees) worn by women from various tribes in the Oaxaca region and by Mayan women. *Serapes* are the blanket-like cloths worn by men, usually slung over the shoulder. Their beautiful designs are woven from wool or cotton in soft colors from natural dyes. The *rebozo* is a long shawl, used to cover a woman's head or hold a baby. Of Spanish origin, this garment is made of wool, cotton, or silk.

Many other folk arts are part of Mexican culture. For example:

Dr. Atl was the pseudonym of Gerardo Murillo, a famous Mexican painter. A teacher at the San Carlos Academy, he believed art was meant to be for the common people.

✳   Mexican leatherwork includes huaraches—sandals of braided leather—and intricately tooled gear for horses, such as bridles and saddles.

✳   Mexican wickerwork comes from places where palms and reeds grow. A petate is an all-purpose mat made of reeds. Pre-Hispanic in origin, it can be used as a seat, a table, or a bed.

✳   Mexican lacquerwork is a craft that originated in pre-Hispanic times. Lacquer chests are some of the most beautiful pieces produced today.

✳   Mexican glassware, though Spanish in origin, is now known for its use of many different colors, especially blue, green, and brown.

Folk artists are young and old, Indian and *mestizo*, from all the different regions of Mexico. Many have other jobs but create folk art for special religious occasions as a way to express their beliefs. Other folk artists work at their craft full time, selling what they produce for the tourist market. They may work in traditional materials or they may incorporate aspects of modern culture into their work. Either way, they are expressing the liveliness and creativity of Mexican culture.

55

CHRONOLOGY

1150–600 B.C.	Olmec culture rises and spreads.
A.D. 100–750	Teotihuacán culture flourishes in the central highlands
300–900	Mayan culture dominates the Yucatán Peninsula.
	The city of Tenochtitlán is founded by the Aztecs.
	Cortés arrives in Mexico and begins his conquest.
1783	San Carlos Academy of Fine Arts is built in the Neoclassical style of architecture.
	Miguel Hidalgo y Castilla begins the War of Independence against Spain.
	José Joaquín Fernández de Lizardi founds the Public Society of Writing to distribute books and newspapers.
	Mexico gains its independence from Spain, ending the colonial era.
1843	The Gran Teatro, a theater for music, dance, and drama, is built in Mexico City.
	Mexico has a new and liberal constitution.
1858–1861	The War of Reform is fought between conservative forces and liberal forces.
	Maximilian, Archduke of Austria, is crowned Emperor of Mexico.
	Liberal armies defeat the Empire. The period of the Renaciamento begins.
1876	Porfirio Díaz seizes power and controls the presidency for the next 34 years, a period often called the Porfiriato.

1910–1921   The Mexican Revolution encouraged Mexican artists to celebrate their history.

The first exhibition of Mexican folk art is organized by Dr. Atl.

1926   Rivera completes his finest mural at the National School of Agriculture.

1952   Amalia Hernández founds the Ballet Folklórico de México.

1990   Mexican poet Octavio Paz wins the Nobel Prize.

2000   Vicente Fox, the candidate for the conservative National Action Party, is elected president. A tolerant political climate allows the arts to flourish.

2002   *Frida*, a film about the life and art of Frida Kahlo, is shown at the Cannes Film Festival.

2005   Francisco Toledo receives the international Right Livelihood Award for humanitarian work.

2006   Carlos Fuentes publishes a new book called *Todas las Familias Felices* (All the Happy Families).

2008   Rufino Tamayo's painting *Trovador* sells for $7.2 million at a New York City auction, setting a new world record for the price of a work of Latin American art.

GLOSSARY

Abstract	In abstract art, artists create images of ideas instead of reflections of objects or people that exist in the real world.
Adobe	Building material made of sun-dried mud and straw.
Aqueducts	Pipes for carrying water.
Arch	A curved structure that spans an opening in a building and serves as support.
Arsenal	A building where weapons and military equipment are stored.
Baroque	A highly ornamental style of European architecture and art that lasted from the mid-16th century to the early 18th century.
Basalt	A hard, black volcanic rock.
Botanist	A person with an expert knowledge of plants.
Cast iron	Iron that is shaped by casting, rather than hammering, often used for decorative fences and window bars.
Cathedrals	A large church that is a bishop's official seat.
Censors	Officials who examine publications for objectionable material.
Choreographers	Artists who direct and arrange the movements of a dance.
Civic	Having to do with the affairs of society.
Complex	A group of buildings that all serve the same purpose.
Conquest	The act or processing of conquering.
Corbel vault	An arch that extends from a wall.
Fiesta	A Spanish party or celebration.
Fresco	A painting on a wall or ceiling made by brushing watercolors onto fresh damp plaster, or onto partly dry plaster.
Grid	A network of squares formed by horizontal and vertical lines.

Mariachi	A Mexican street band with a distinctive type of music.
Medieval	The period of European history from about A.D. 500 to about 1500.
Mestizo	A person of mixed European and Native American heritage.
Mosaics	Wall or floor decorations made by inlaying small pieces of colored materials to form pictures or patterns.
Muralist	A person who paints a large work of art on a wall.
Neoclassical	In architecture, an 18th- and 19th-century revival of the simple, symmetrical building styles of ancient Greece and Rome.
Parapets	Low walls or railings.
Peasants	Laborers who belong to a lower social class.
Plazas	An open public square in a city or town.
Pre-Hispanic	The period before the Spaniards arrived in Mexico.

FURTHER READING

Coe, Michael D., and Rex Koontz. *Mexico: From the Olmecs to the Aztecs*. New York: Thames and Hudson, 2008.

Hamnet, Brian R. *A Concise History of Mexico*. New York: Cambridge University Press, 2006.

Herrera, Hayden, et al. *Frida Kahlo*. Minneapolis: Walker Art Center, 2007.

Joseph, Gilbert M., editor. *The Mexico Reader: History, Culture, Politics*. Durham, N.C.: Duke University Press, 2002.

Lozano, Luis Martin, and Juan Coronel Rivera. *Diego Rivera: The Complete Murals*. New York: Taschen, 2008.

McMenamin, Donna, and Richard Loper. *Popular Arts of Mexico: 1850–1950*. Schiffer Publishing, 2000.

Mayor, Guy. *Mexico: A Quick Guide to Customs and Etiquette*. New York: Kuperard, 2006.

Orellana, Margarita de. *Crafts of Mexico*. Washington, D.C.: Smithsonian, 2004.

Rothstein, Arden Aibel. *Mexican Folk Art*. Atglen, Pa.: Schiffer Publishing, 2007.

Williams, Colleen Madonna Flood. *The People of Mexico*. Philadelphia: Mason Crest, 2009.

INTERNET RESOURCES

Artist Profile: Frida Kahlo
http://www.nmwa.org/legacy/bios/bkahlo.htm

Mexico Connect
http://www.mexconnect.com

Mexico Online
http://www.mexonline.com/history.htm

Mexico Reference Desk
http://lanic.utexas.edu/la/Mexico

The Sor Juana Inés de la Cruz Project
http://www.dartmouth.edu/~sorjuana

The Virtual Diego Rivera Web Museum
http://www.diegorivera.com/

Publisher's Note: The websites listed on this page were active at the time of publication. The publisher is not responsible for websites that have changed their address or discontinued operation since the date of publication. The publisher reviews and updates the websites each time the book is reprinted.

INDEX

PICTURE CREDITS

2:	IMS Communications, Ltd.	39:	Corbis Images
10:	Dallas and John Heaton/Corbis	40:	Hulton/Archive
13:	Danny Lehman/Corbis	43:	Christopher Cormack/Corbis
14:	Randy Faris/Corbis	44:	Archivo Iconografico, S.A./Corbis
17:	Corbis Images	47:	Fulvio Roiter/Corbis
18:	IMS Communications, Ltd.	48:	Charles and Josette Lenars/Corbis
20:	Hulton/Archive	50:	The Purcell Team/Corbis
23:	Hulton/Archive	51:	The Purcell Team/Corbis
24:	Hulton/Archive	52:	IMS Communications, Ltd
27:	Hulton-Deutsch Collection/Corbis	55:	Bettmann/Corbis
28:	Corbis Images		
32:	Owen Franken/Corbis	Cover:	(front - all) Used under license from
35:	David Seawell/Corbis		Shutterstock, Inc.; (back) Used under
36:	Lindsay Hebberd/Corbis		license from Shutterstock, Inc.

63

CONTRIBUTORS

Roger E. Hernández is the most widely syndicated columnist writing on Hispanic issues in the United States. His weekly column, distributed by King Features, appears in some 40 newspapers across the country, including the *Washington Post*, *Los Angeles Daily News*, *Dallas Morning News*, *Arizona Republic*, *Rocky Mountain News* in Denver, *El Paso Times*, and *Hartford Courant*. He is also the author of *Cubans in America*, an illustrated history of the Cuban presence in what is now the United States, from the early colonists in 16th-century Florida to today's Castro-era exiles. The book was designed to accompany a PBS documentary of the same title.

Hernández's articles and essays have been published in the *New York Times*, *New Jersey Monthly*, *Reader's Digest*, and *Vista Magazine*; he is a frequent guest on television and radio political talk shows, and often travels the country to lecture on his topic of expertise. Currently, he is teaching journalism and English composition at the New Jersey Institute of Technology in Newark, where he holds the position of writer-in-residence. He is also a member of the adjunct faculty at Rutgers University.

Hernández left Cuba with his parents at the age of nine. After living in Spain for a year, the family settled in Union City, New Jersey, where Hernández grew up. He attended Rutgers University, where he earned a BA in Journalism in 1977; after graduation, he worked in television news before moving to print journalism in 1983. He lives with his wife and two children in Upper Montclair, New Jersey.

Anna Carew-Miller is a freelance writer and former teacher. She lives in rural Connecticut with her husband, her daughter, and a very large cat. They enjoy hiking, backpacking, and cross-country skiing. Anna has a B.A. in English from the College of William and Mary, an M.A. in English from Yale University, and a Ph.D. in American Literature from the University of New Mexico. She has done extensive research and writing on women in literature, nature writing, and Native American literature.